CD-ALF-384

Salad Time

Salad Time

Over 260 Original and
Unique Salad Recipes

THE JUDAICA PRESS, INC.

Salad Time
© 2007 The Judaica Press, Inc.

Other books by this author: Salad Time 2

All rights reserved. No part of this publication may be
translated, reproduced, stored in a retrieval system
or transmitted in any form or by any means, electronic,
mechanical, photocopying, recording or otherwise,
without permission in writing from the publisher.

ISBN: 978-1-932443-66-0

Proofreader: Hadassa Goldsmith
Cover design and layout: Justine Elliott

THE JUDAICA PRESS, INC.
123 Ditmas Avenue / Brooklyn, NY 11218
718-972-6200 / 800-972-6201
info@judaicapress.com
www.judaicapress.com

Manufactured in the United States of America

Contents

Vegetable Salads

Vegetable Salads

Arugula Salad

1 (10-oz.) pkg. arugula salad
1 T. crushed garlic
1 T. dill
1 T. mustard
1 T. apple cider vinegar
2 T. olive oil

Mix garlic, dill and mustard. Slowly add in vinegar and olive oil. Mix well. Pour dressing over salad right before serving.

Arugula Salad

1 (10-oz.) bag romaine lettuce
1 (10-oz.) bag arugula leaves
½ box fresh mushrooms
1 box grape tomatoes

Dressing:
2/3 c. olive oil
2 tsp. sugar
1 tsp. salt
2 tsp. mustard
¼ tsp. black pepper
¼ c. lemon juice

Whisk together all dressing ingredients. Pour over salad right before serving.

Asparagus Salad

1 lb. asparagus, ends trimmed
1 T. olive oil
1 tsp. crushed garlic
Dash salt & black pepper

Place asparagus in pot of salted water. Bring to a boil and cook for 5 minutes. Drain and remove. Mix in oil and spices. Can serve warm or cold.

Avocado Salad

1 avocado, cubed
1 can hearts of palm, sliced
1 box cherry tomatoes, cut in half

Dressing:
½ c. mayonnaise
2 T. lemon juice
Onion powder & salt to taste

Place avocado, hearts of palm and tomatoes in bowl. Pour dressing over and mix well.

Avocado Corn Relish

4 c. corn
¾ c. olive oil
1 tsp. salt
¾ tsp. black pepper
2 avocados, cubed
1 red pepper, diced
4 poblano chilies, roasted, peeled & seeded
4 scallions, thinly sliced
½ c. vinegar

Heat ½ cup olive oil in pot and sauté corn for 2 minutes.
Mix in salt and black pepper and stir for 5 minutes.
Place in bowl to cool. Add remaining ingredients to corn.
Marinate for 20-30 minutes before serving.

Bean Salad

½ bag pinto beans
½ bag lima beans
3 T. mayonnaise
3 T. ketchup
1 tsp. mustard
3 dashes Worcestershire sauce
Salt, pepper & paprika to taste
2 scallions, diced
2 celery, diced
2 green peppers, diced

Place beans in pot of water. Bring to a boil. Simmer for
2 minutes and drain. Mix rest of ingredients in bowl and
add beans. Marinate for 1 hour before serving.

Bean Salad

2 (15-oz.) cans dark kidney beans, drained
½ c. diced onions
3 gherkin pickles, diced
4 hard-boiled eggs, diced
2 T. cider vinegar
½ c. onions, diced
2-3 T. sugar

Combine all ingredients. Keep refrigerated until ready to serve.

Three Bean Salad

1 can wax beans, drained
1 can regular green beans, drained
1 can chickpeas, drained
1 red pepper, diced
5-6 scallions, chopped
Little less than ½ c. vinegar
¼-½ c. sugar
¼ c. oil

Combine all ingredients. Marinate 2-3 days.

Beet Salad

2 cans sliced beets, drained
1 sm. onion, sliced into rings
2/3 c. vinegar
½ tsp. black pepper
2 T. horseradish
½ c. sugar
1 tsp. salt

Combine all ingredients in bowl. Marinate overnight.

Bodek Salad

1 Bodek lettuce salad mix
2 sour pickles, cubed
2 scallions, diced
½ green & red pepper, diced

Dressing:
¾ c. mayonnaise
½ c. sugar
¼ c. vinegar
1 tsp. salt
Dash garlic powder & black pepper

Combine ingredients in bowl.

Bok Choy Salad

2 (3-oz.) pkgs. Oriental flavor Ramen noodles
¾ c. sugar
¾ c. olive oil
⅓ c. white vinegar
2 T. soy sauce
3 head bok choy
2 bunches scallions, chopped
1 jar sunflower seeds
3 c. sliced almonds

Remove seasoning packets from Ramen noodles and set noodles aside. Combine seasonings, sugar, oil, vinegar and soy sauce in jar. Cover and shake well. Slice bok choy into bite-size including stems. Combine bok choy, scallions, sunflower seeds and almonds in large bowl. Add dressing and noodles right before serving.

Broccoli Salad

l-lb. bag broccoli (bite-size)
Handful plain cashew nuts
Handful craisins
1 red onion, diced

Dressing:
1 c. mayonnaise
¼ c. lemon juice
2 T. sugar

Combine dressing; pour over salad ingredients. Mix well.

Broccoli Salad

1 lb. broccoli florets
1 red onion, diced
1 carrot, diced
½ c. raisins
½ c. sunflower seeds
½ c. unsalted cashews

Dressing:
¾ c. mayonnaise
⅓ c. red wine vinegar
¼ c. sugar

Mix together dressing ingredients. Pour over salad and mix well.

Broccoli & Avocado Salad

1 box cherry tomatoes, cut in half
1 avocado, cubed
1 (1-lb.) bunch broccoli (bite-size)
1 bag shredded purple cabbage

Dressing:
1 bottle lite Italian dressing

Pour dressing over salad ingredients; place avocado cubes on salad right before serving.

Broccoli Craisin Salad

2 lbs. frozen broccoli (bite-size), thawed
1 box craisins
1 med. purple onion, diced
1 c. roasted slivered almonds

Dressing:
2/3 c. mayonnaise
4 T. sugar
4 T. lemon juice

Mix together dressing ingredients. Pour over salad ingredients before serving.

Vegetable Salads

Broccoli with Garlic & Oil

1 lb. broccoli florets
2-3 garlic cloves, chopped
5-6 T. olive oil
Salt & black pepper

Place broccoli in pot of water; boil 5–10 minutes. Drain. Heat garlic in oil; add broccoli, turning side to side for
5 minutes. Remove. Season with salt and black pepper.

Broccoli Tomato Salad

1 lg. bunch broccoli florets
¾ c. sliced fresh mushrooms
2 lg. tomatoes, cut in wedges
2 green onions, sliced

Dressing:
¾ c. olive oil
⅓ c. tarragon vinegar
2 T. water
1 tsp. lemon juice
1 tsp. sugar
1 tsp. salt
¾ tsp. dried thyme
1 garlic clove, crushed
½ tsp. celery seed
¼ tsp. Italian seasoning
¼ tsp. lemon pepper seasoning
¼ tsp. paprika
¼ tsp. ground dry mustard

Place broccoli in small pot of water. Cook for 5 minutes. Drain; rinse with cold water. Combine broccoli with tomatoes, mushrooms and onions. Pour dressing over vegetables. Chill for 1 hour.

Cabbage Salad

½ bag coleslaw
1 bag radishes, sliced
2 carrots, sliced

Dressing:
2-4 T. mayonnaise
¼ c. vinegar
Dash salt, black pepper & sugar

Pour dressing over vegetables and refrigerate.

Cabbage & Peanut Salad

¼ c. smooth peanut butter
½ c. boiling water
¼ c. apple cider vinegar
3 T. brown sugar
1 T. tamari soy sauce
1 tsp. sesame oil
1 tsp. salt
8 c. green cabbage
¼ tsp. crushed red pepper
½ c. roasted, unsalted peanuts, shelled & red skins removed

In large bowl, mix the peanut butter and boiling water
together until smooth. Add vinegar, brown sugar, tamari, oil
and salt, blending together well. Stir in cabbage about two
cups at a time, mixing well to coat evenly. Add the red pepper.
Cover bowl tightly and refrigerate for 12-24 hours.

Just before serving, transfer to a serving dish with a slotted
spoon and sprinkle peanuts on top.

Green Cabbage Salad

1 (16-oz.) bag green cabbage, shredded
2 carrots, sliced
1 onion, sliced
2 cucumbers, sliced

Dressing:
¾ c. vinegar
½ c. sugar
4 tsp. salt
2 tsp. lemon juice
½ c. olive oil

Mix dressing and pour over salad.

Marinated Cabbage Salad

1 (16-oz.) bag shredded green cabbage
1 (10-oz.) bag shredded purple cabbage
3 baby squash
1 box cherry tomatoes
2 purple onions, chopped
4 different colored peppers (red, orange, green & yellow)

Dressing:
¾ c. oil
¾ c. vinegar
¾ c. sugar
2 T. salt

Place cabbage in bowl, slice onions in circle, cube squash, shred carrots and slice peppers. Pour dressing over. Marinate for 2 days. Place cherry tomatoes on salad right before serving.

Purple & Green Cabbage Salad

1 bag shredded purple cabbage
1 bag shredded lettuce
2 kirbys, sliced or diced
Handful sunflower seeds
Chow mein noodles

Dressing:
½ c. oil
5-6 T. brown sugar
4 T. vinegar
Less than 1 tsp. salt
Dash black pepper

Mix together dressing. Combine cabbage, lettuce and kirbys in bowl. Pour dressing over. Mix well. Place seeds and chow mein on top.

Purple & White Cabbage Salad

½ bag shredded purple cabbage
½ bag shredded white cabbage
3 carrots, shredded
1 red pepper, sliced

Dressing:
½ c. vinegar
¼ c. oil
2 scallions, sliced
1 garlic clove, minced
5 T. mayonnaise
5 T. sugar
1 tsp. salt

Mix dressing well. Pour over salad ingredients right before serving.

Vegetable Salads

Red Cabbage Salad

2 bags shredded purple cabbage
2 bunches scallions, sliced
1 c. chow mein noodles

Dressing:
½ c. oil
1 T. salt
¼ c. water
½ c. sugar
5 T. vinegar

Whisk dressing well. Pour over salad ingredients before serving.
Garnish with chow mein noodles.

2-Tone Cabbage Salad

2 bags shredded green cabbage
1 bunch (5-6) carrots, grated on long side

Dressing:
⅔ c. sugar
⅔ c. vinegar
3-4 T. mayonnaise

Pour dressing over cabbage and carrots. Marinate for 1 hour.

Caesar Salad

1 bag romaine lettuce

Dressing:
¼ c. olive oil
1 heaping tsp. crushed garlic
1 tsp. lemon juice
3 T. mayonnaise
1 T. sugar
1 T. dry parsley
1 tsp. dry chives
½ tsp. dry mustard
1 box croutons

Mix together dressing ingredients. Pour over salad right before
serving. Add croutons on top.

Caesar Salad

1 bag shredded lettuce, or 1 head lettuce
¼ c. vinegar
½ tsp. salt
1 c. mayonnaise
1 T. crushed garlic (in oil)
1 red onion, sliced

Mix together vinegar, mayonnaise, salt and garlic; pour over lettuce and sliced onion; add croutons on top.

Caesar Salad

1 bag romaine lettuce
1 red onion, thinly sliced
1 box cherry tomatoes
1 c. croutons

Dressing:
½ c. mayonnaise
¾ c. olive oil
1 T. sugar
¾ tsp. black pepper
1 T. dry mustard
½ tsp. soy sauce
¼ tsp. lemon juice
1 tsp. crushed garlic

Mix together dressing ingredients. Pour over salad right before serving. Place croutons on top.

Vegetable Salads

Caesar Salad

1 **bag romaine lettuce**
Parmesan cheese, grated
½ **box mushrooms, sliced**
½ **box cherry tomatoes, cut in half**
1 **c. croutons**

Dressing:
1 **egg**
½ **tsp. black pepper**
4 **T. sugar**
½ **tsp. oregano**
1 **tsp. salt**
¼ **tsp. dried mustard**
1 **tsp. Worcestershire sauce**
2-3 **garlic cloves, crushed**
½ **c. vinegar**
1 **c. oil**
¼ **c. mayonnaise**

Run egg under hot water for one minute; process all dressing ingredients in food processor, slowly adding oil. Pour dressing over romaine lettuce, mushrooms and cherry tomatoes. Sprinkle with Parmesan cheese; add croutons on top.

Caesar Salad

1 (10-oz.) **bag lettuce or romaine lettuce**
1 **c. croutons**

Dressing:
1 **c. mayonnaise**
¼ **c. sugar**
¼ **c. vinegar**
Handful dill seed
2 **cloves garlic, crushed**

Mix together dressing ingredients. Pour over salad before serving. Add croutons on top.

Caesar Salad

1 bag lettuce, shredded
1 box sesame rye croutons

Dressing:
¼ c. sugar
¼ c. vinegar
¼ c. water
1 c. mayonnaise
Dash garlic powder

Put dressing in blender; pour over lettuce before serving.
Add croutons on top.

Baby Carrots

1 bag baby carrots
2 T. butter or margarine
1 tsp. salt

Place carrots in pot with enough water to cover. Add salt; bring
to a boil (10 minutes). Put carrots in bowl. Season with salt and
butter. Serve warm.

Carrot Salad

4 carrots, peeled and cut in strips

Dressing:
¼ c. olive oil
1 tsp. crushed garlic
1 T. lemon juice
Salt & black pepper to taste

Put carrot strips in bowl, add dressing and mix well.

Carrot Salad

1 bag carrots, peeled
2 cloves garlic, crushed
2 T. oil
2 T. lemon juice
Dash salt, cumin, white pepper & paprika

Slice carrots and boil in pot until tender. Mix in rest of ingredients. Serve warm.

Carrot & Pea Salad

1 (15-oz.) can peas, drained
1 (15-oz.) can carrots, drained
1 tomato, diced
1 sour pickle, diced
4 scallions, sliced
½ cup mayonnaise
Dash black pepper

Mix first five ingredients in bowl. Add mayonnaise and black pepper. Mix well.

Cashew-Radicchio Salad

1 bag Italian lettuce blend
1 lb. frozen broccoli florets, thawed
1 c. roasted cashews
½ c. craisins
1 sm. purple onion, sliced

Dressing:
⅓ c. red wine vinegar
1 c. mayonnaise
¼ c. sugar
1 T. lemon juice

Combine lettuce, broccoli, cashews and craisins in bowl. Add onion to dressing and mix well in salad.

Cauliflower Salad

1 head cauliflower, cut in bite-size pieces
4 baby squash, sliced
1 green pepper, diced
1 box cherry tomatoes, cut in half

 Dressing:
½ - ¾ c. vinegar
¼ c. sugar
½ c. oil
1 tsp. sweet basil
1 tsp. salt
½ tsp. black pepper

Cook cauliflower and squash in pot of water for 2 minutes. Drain and remove. Pour dressing over cauliflower, squash, pepper and tomatoes. Let stand for 24 hours. Toss occasionally.

Cauliflower Salad

1 whole cauliflower (bite-size)
6 sour pickles, diced
1 carrot, grated
1 carrot, sliced
1 green pepper, sliced
1 c. mayonnaise
½ c. pickle juice
¼ c. vinegar

Cook cauliflower in salted water for 15 minutes. Drain. Combine with rest of ingredients. Chill before serving.

Celery & Carrot Salad

1 bunch celery, sliced
1 bag carrots, shredded
1 red onion, diced
2 green peppers, diced

Dressing:
½ c. oil
¼ c. vinegar
½ c. sugar
1 tsp. salt
½ c. mayonnaise

Mix dressing well. Add to vegetables right before serving.

Chickpea Salad

1 ctn. fresh chickpeas
1 red onion, diced
1 box cherry tomatoes, cut in half
1 bottle coleslaw dressing (store bought)

Pour dressing over vegetables and mix well.

Chickpea Salad

2 cans chickpeas, drained
5 scallions, chopped
2 tomatoes, cubed
1 c. black olives, sliced
Handful fresh parsley

Dressing:
5 T. olive oil
3 T. wine vinegar
Salt & black pepper

Combine vegetables in bowl. Pour dressing over. Marinate for 1 hour before serving.

Chinese Salad

1 bag shredded lettuce
1 bunch scallions, chopped
1 c. chow mein noodles
1 can water chestnuts, drained
1 c. cashew nuts
¼ c. roasted sesame seed

Dressing:
1 T. dried onion
1 tsp. dry mustard
1 tsp. salt
½ c. oil
½ c. sugar
½ c. cider vinegar

Combine together all vegetables in bowl. Pour dressing over salad just before serving.

Classic Coleslaw

6 c. shredded cabbage
1 c. shredded carrots
½ c. thinly sliced green peppers

Dressing:
1 c. mayonnaise
3 T. lemon juice
2 T. sugar
1 tsp. salt

Combine dressing ingredients; stir in remaining vegetables. Cover and chill in refrigerator.

Creamy Coleslaw

1 bag coleslaw

Dressing:
½ c. mayonnaise
2 T. parve milk
1 T. white vinegar
½ tsp. sugar

Pour dressing over coleslaw mix. Let stand in refrigerator for 1 hour and then serve.

Coleslaw

1 bag Bodek cabbage, shredded
½ c. shredded carrots

Dressing:
1 tsp. salt
4-5 T. mayonnaise
½ c. water
¼ c. vinegar
¾ c. sugar

Combine dressing; pour over cabbage and carrots. Marinate overnight.

Coleslaw

2 bags coleslaw

Dressing:
¾ c. mayonnaise
¾ c. sugar
¼ c. water
⅛ c. lemon juice
½ tsp. salt

Combine ingredients for dressing. Pour over cabbage. Mix well and chill.

Diet Coleslaw

2 bags Bodek coleslaw

 Dressing:
2 T. vinegar
2 T. lemon juice
1 c. hot water
5 T. mayonnaise
4 pkgs. Equal
Dash salt

Mix dressing well; pour over coleslaw. Marinate in refrigerator overnight.

Different Coleslaw

1 bag coleslaw

 Dressing:
¼ c. olive oil
1 tsp. salt
Black pepper
2 T. red wine vinegar

Mix dressing; add to cabbage before serving.

Oriental Coleslaw

1 bag coleslaw
½ red onion, diced
Chinese noodles

 Dressing:
½ c. oil
6 T. sugar
6 T. vinegar
½ tsp. salt
½ tsp. black pepper

Combine coleslaw and onion. Add dressing right before serving and top with chinese noodles.

Cool Zucchini Slaw

3 med. zucchinis, grated
1 med. sweet onion, thinly sliced
1 ½ tsp. coarse salt
1 sm. red pepper, diced
¼ c. cider vinegar
2 T. chopped fresh basil

Place zucchinis and onion in a colander. Set over a bowl. Add salt and toss. Let drain for ½ hour, rinse and squeeze. Add rest of ingredients and mix well.

Zucchini Slaw

2 zucchinis, shredded
1 carrot, shredded
3 T. vinegar
2 T. sugar
2 T. mayonnaise

Mix all ingredients and chill.

Colorful Vinaigrette

8 med. beets
3 med. potatoes
5 carrots
1 c. sour pickles, cubed
1 med. onion, diced
½ c. oil
Dash lemon juice, salt & black pepper

Peel beets. Boil in pot of water. Add unpeeled potatoes and carrots; cook until soft. Peel potatoes and carrots. Combine with rest of ingredients.

Colorful Veggie Salad

2 zucchinis
2 kirbys
1 pkg. snow peas
1 box cherry tomatoes
1 c. black olives
1 red pepper
1 can whole mushrooms, drained
Carrots

Dressing
¾ c. white vinegar
½ c. oil
3 T. water
¾ c. sugar
2 ½ tsp. salt

Slice and dice vegetables and layer in trifle bowl. Pour dressing over salad when ready to serve.

Corn Salad

2 (11-oz.) cans corn, drained
2 hot green peppers, thinly cut
1 c. grape tomatoes
Hard salami, thinly sliced
½ T. wine vinegar
1 ½ T. olive oil
1 T. fresh chopped basil
1 clove garlic, minced
Salt & black pepper

Mix all ingredients together well. Serve with thin slices of hard salami.

Vegetable Salads

Corn Salad

1 (11-oz.) can corn, drained
2 tomatoes
2 kirbys
1 red pepper
1 green pepper
½ bottle coleslaw dressing (store bought)

Dice all vegetables except for corn, then add to corn. Pour coleslaw dressing over corn. Mix well.

Corn Salad

1 (11-oz.) can corn, drained
2 sour pickles, diced
1 tomato, diced
2 T. mayonnaise
Dash garlic powder, onion powder & salt

Mix vegetables in bowl. Combine with mayonnaise and spices.

Corn Salad

1 (11-oz.) can corn, drained
1 kirby, diced
2 sour pickles, diced
1 red onion, diced
3 T. oil
½ tsp. salt
Juice of 1 lemon
Handful dill

Combine together all ingredients. Mix well and chill.

Baby Corn Salad

2 cans baby corn, cut in half
1 pkg. frozen snap peas, thawed
1 green pepper, cut in strips
1 red pepper, cut in strips
1 yellow pepper, cut in strips
1 orange pepper, cut in strips
1 red onion, thinly sliced

 Dressing:
2 ¹/₃ c. oil
2 ¹/₃ c. vinegar
2 ¹/₃ c. sugar
4 T. water
4 tsp. salt

Pour dressing over salad. Mix well. Marinate overnight.

Sweet Corn Salad

2 cans sweet corn, drained
2 cans peas, drained
1 yellow pepper, diced
1 red pepper, diced
1 green pepper, diced
1 orange pepper, diced
1 purple onion, diced

 Dressing:
¼ c. oil
1 c. sugar
¼ c. water
Salt & pepper to taste

Combine all vegetables in bowl, pour over dressing and mix well.

Corn Relish

1 lg. can corn, drained
1 chopped tomato
1 can chickpeas, drained
¼ c. Italian dressing

Combine together all ingredients. Mix well.

Corn & Pea Salad

2 (15-oz.) cans corn, drained
¼ c. frozen peas
¼ c. water
1 ½ c. chopped plum tomatoes
2 T. chopped fresh basil
2 T. chives
1 T. margarine or butter
¼ tsp. salt
¼ tsp. black pepper

Place corn and peas in pot of water. Cook for 2 ½ minutes.
Combine rest of ingredients with corn and peas. Serve hot or cold.

Corn & Pea Salad

2 (15-oz.) cans peas, drained
2 (15-oz.) cans white shoe peg corn, drained
1 can sliced water chestnuts, drained
1 yellow pepper, diced very small
1 red pepper, diced very small
1 green pepper, diced very small
1 red onion, diced very small

Dressing:
¾ c. oil
1 c. water
1 c. sugar
½ c. vinegar
1 tsp. salt
½ tsp. black pepper

Combine vegetables in bowl, pour over dressing right before
serving and mix well.

Imitation Crab Salad

1 pkg. imitation crabmeat
1 stalk celery
1 red pepper
1 green pepper
1 orange pepper
1 yellow pepper
2 kirbys
1 purple onion, diced
½ c. mayonnaise
Dash salt

Cut crabmeat in pieces; chop celery, peppers, kirbys and onion.
Mix well; add mayonnaise and salt

Crunchy Euro Salad

1 bag euro mix
1 red onion, diced
1 box grape tomatoes

Dressing:
⅓ c. mayonnaise
⅓ c. vinegar
3 T. olive oil
Dash black pepper and garlic powder

Combine vegetables in bowl. Pour over dressing right
before serving.

Cucumber Salad

6 kirbys, peeled & sliced
1 med. onion, thinly sliced
1 tsp. salt
⅓ c. mayonnaise
2 T. mustard
½ tsp. dill weed

Place kirbys in bowl with onion and salt for ½ hour.
Remove kirbys; squeeze out any excess water. Add
remaining ingredients and toss well.

Cucumber Salad

6 cucumbers, peeled & sliced

 Dressing:
½ c. vinegar
2 med. onions, sliced
Dash salt
½ c. sugar

Salt cucumbers; let stand for 1 hour. Drain and mix
with dressing.

Cucumber Salad

2 cucumbers or 4 kirbys, peeled & sliced
¼ c. sugar
1 T. lemon juice
1 sm. onion, minced
½ tsp. salt
¼ tsp. dill

Combine all ingredients in bowl. Marinate for 1 day.

Kirby Salad

4 kirbys, sliced in circles
1 red onion, sliced
1 green pepper, thinly sliced
2 red peppers, thinly sliced
2 yellow peppers, thinly sliced

Dressing:
¼ c. water
A little less than ¾ c. sugar
½ c. vinegar
½ c. oil
3 T. salt

Combine kirbys, onion and peppers in bowl. Pour dressing
over vegetables. Marinate for 2 days.

Eggplant Salad

3 lg. onions, sliced
3 lg. eggplants, cubed
½ clove garlic, minced
1 red pepper, chopped
4 scallions, sliced

Dressing:
1 c. ketchup
½ c. vinegar
Salt & black pepper to taste

Place onions with 1 teaspoon salt in large frying pan. Sauté in oil for a few minutes. Toss in rest of ingredients to onions until soft. Combine dressing ingredients to mixture. Let simmer 5-10 minutes on low flame.

Baked Eggplant

1 lg. eggplant
1 red pepper
1 yellow pepper
1 T. sugar
1 T. lemon juice
Dash salt, black pepper & oil
1 tsp. crushed garlic

Slice eggplant; sprinkle oil and salt. Bake at 400° until brown. Peel red and yellow peppers; sprinkle oil, salt and black pepper. Bake at 400° until soft. Mix eggplant and peppers in bowl. Combine with sugar, lemon juice and garlic.

Israeli Eggplant Salad

2 eggplants, peeled & cubed
I tsp. salt
¾ c. oil
¼ c. red pepper
¼ c. green pepper

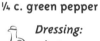

Dressing:
2 hot peppers
¼ c. ketchup
1 T. sugar
3 T. vinegar
2 cloves garlic

Sprinkle salt and oil on eggplants and bake 45 minutes to
1 hour at 400°. Dice red and green peppers and add to
eggplant. Combine dressing ingredients in blender. Pour over
eggplants and peppers.

Endive Salad

1 head lettuce, shredded
3 endives, thinly sliced
1 bunch scallions, sliced
1 bunch radishes, sliced
1 T. lemon juice
1 T. olive oil
Salt & black pepper

Combine all ingredients in bowl. Mix well.

Everyday Salad

½ bag shredded lettuce
2 tomatoes
2 green peppers
2 red peppers
2 kirbys
3 sour pickles

Dressing:
2 oz. pickle juice
1 oz. olive oil
Pinch salt & garlic powder
Juice of 1 lemon

Dice all vegetables; add to lettuce. Pour dressing over right
before serving.

Flatbread Salad

2 bags euro salad
1 box cherry tomatoes, cut in half
½ pkg. flatbreads, crushed
2 hard boiled eggs, sliced

Dressing:
1 garlic clove, crushed
1 T. sugar
¾ c. oil
½ tsp. soy sauce
¼ tsp. vinegar
1 tsp. mustard
1 tsp. black pepper
1 tsp. salt

Mix salad, crushed flatbreads, tomatoes and eggs in bowl. Pour
dressing over right before serving.

Garden Salad

1 red pepper, cut in strips
1 green pepper, cut in strips
1 yellow pepper, cut in strips
1 purple onion, cut in circles
2 baby squash, cut in semi-circles
2 carrots, cut in circles
1 can baby corn, drained

Dressing:
½ c. sugar
½ c. vinegar
½ c. water
⅓ c. oil
1 tsp. salt
Salad herbs

Combine all ingredients in large bowl. Marinate a few hours before serving.

Green Salad

1 bag salad leaves
1 cucumber, sliced
2 tomatoes, sliced
1 bunch radishes, sliced
½ c. black olives
2 hard boiled eggs, sliced
4 oz. green beans
1 c. fresh parsley

Dressing:
6 T. oil
1 T. crushed garlic
1 T. white wine vinegar
Dash salt & black pepper

Combine all ingredients in bowl. Mix in dressing. Sprinkle parsley over salad right before serving.

Green Beans in Tomato Sauce

1 med. onion, diced
2 T. water
Oil
1 (8-oz.) can tomato sauce
1 (16-oz.) can green beans, drained

Sauté onion in oil; add tomato sauce and water. Bring to a boil; add green beans. On low flame, cook vegetables for 10 minutes.

Green Bean & Pepper Salad

1 bag iceberg lettuce
12 oz. cooked green beans
2 red peppers, diced
2 scallions, chopped
1 c. sliced green olives

Dressing:
3 T. red wine vinegar
8 T. olive oil
Salt & black pepper

Combine green beans, peppers and scallions in bowl. Pour dressing over salad. Mix well. Place lettuce in a big bowl. Pour vegetables on top of lettuce. Garnish with olives.

Green Bean & Squash Salad

2 lbs. green beans
2 lbs. yellow squash

Dressing:
½ c. vinegar
¾ c. oil
¼ tsp. garlic powder
⅛ tsp. dill weed
Dash paprika, salt & black pepper

Cut green beans and boil in pot 10–12 minutes. Slice squash and boil in pot 5 minutes. Combine green beans and squash in bowl. Pour dressing over and marinate 3-4 hours.

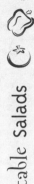

Green Bean & Tomato Salad

1 lb. green beans
3 T. olive oil
1 red onion, sliced
2 plum tomatoes, peeled & chopped
½ c. water
Dash salt & black pepper
Fresh basil

Heat oil in frying pan; add onion; sauté until soft. Add tomatoes. Cook for 8 minutes. Pour water in pan; season with spices; stir in beans. Cover pan and cook 15-20 minutes.

Health Salad

4 cucumbers
3 carrots
1 green & orange pepper, thinly sliced
1 red & yellow pepper, thinly sliced
1 red onion, sliced

 Dressing:
6 pkgs. Equal
½ c. hot water
½ c. vinegar
⅛ c. oil
2 tsp. salt

Slice all vegetables in bowl. Mix dressing ingredients and pour over salad.

Health Salad

1 bag Bodek coleslaw
2 kirbys, sliced
1 pepper, diced
1 carrot, sliced
1 red onion, sliced & separated into rings
1 ½ tsp. salt
¾ c. sugar
¾ c. vinegar
¾ c. oil

Combine all ingredients in one bowl. Marinate overnight.

Health Salad

1 bunch celery, sliced
1 bunch carrots, sliced
2 green peppers, sliced
1 med. purple onion, cut into thin rings

 Dressing:
¼ c. oil
¼ c. sugar
¼ c. mayonnaise
½ c. vinegar
1-2 tsp. salt

Mix dressing well and pour over salad before serving.

Health Salad

1 bag shredded Bodek purple cabbage
1 bag shredded Bodek green cabbage
1 tsp. olive oil
1 tsp. salt
1 yellow pepper, chopped
1 red pepper, chopped
2 med. cucumbers, chopped
1 med. onion, sliced
1 lg. carrot, sliced in circles
1 T. chopped garlic
½ tsp. black pepper

 Dressing:
2 quarts water
1 c. white vinegar
1 lb. sugar

Place cabbages in large bowl. Sprinkle oil and salt, mixing well.
Add peppers, cucumber, onion, carrot, garlic and black pepper
to cabbage. Mix well. Prepare the dressing by combining the
water, vinegar and sugar, stirring well to dissolve the sugar.
Pour over cabbage mixture. Cover bowl and refrigerate for 24
hours before serving.

Hearts of Palm Salad

1 bag lettuce mix
1 pkg. snow peas
1 can hearts of palm, drained and sliced
1 can water chestnuts, drained
1 red pepper, sliced
1 can mushrooms, sliced

 Dressing:
½ c. olive oil
½ c. vinegar
Dash oregano, salt & black pepper

Place lettuce in bowl. Combine rest of vegetables with dressing and pour on top of lettuce.

Israeli Salad

1 bunch chopped fresh parsley
4 kirbys, chopped finely
4 tomatoes, chopped finely
1 bunch scallions, sliced
2 sour pickles, diced
2 T. olive oil
2 tsp. lemon juice
Dash salt, black pepper, garlic powder & cumin

Combine vegetables in bowl. Pour dressing over right before serving.

Layered Salad

1 bag romaine lettuce
1 bag iceberg lettuce
4 hard-boiled eggs, sliced
1 c. fresh mushrooms, sliced
1 red onion, sliced
½ pkg. peas
½ c. mayonnaise
1 T. sugar
Dash salt & black pepper

Place layer of romaine and iceberg on bottom of trifle bowl.
Sprinkle sugar with a little salt and black pepper on top. Layer
eggs, then mushrooms; add lettuce, red onion and then peas.
Cover top of salad with mayonnaise. Put in refrigerator to
marinate for 1 hour.

Lettuce Salad

1 whole lettuce, shredded
1 red onion, sliced in circles
1 c. sliced mushrooms

Dressing:
½ c. olive oil
¼ c. red wine vinegar
1 tsp. salt
¼ tsp. black pepper
¼ tsp. oregano

Mix dressing well and pour over salad.

Lettuce Salad

1 bag lettuce, shredded
1 cucumber, sliced
1 pepper, sliced
2-3 T. olive oil
1 T. balsamic vinegar
Dash salt & black pepper

Combine all ingredients. Mix well.

Lettuce Salad

1 bag lettuce mix
2 cloves garlic, crushed
2 T. mayonnaise
1 T. lemon juice
Salt & black pepper

Combine all ingredients together in bowl.

Lite Salad

1 bag shredded lettuce
1 head cauliflower, cut in bite-size pieces
1 pkg. baby carrots, cut in half
1 pkg. frozen peas, thawed
¾ c. lite mayonnaise
¼ c. vinegar
2 pkgs. NutraSweet

Combine together all ingredients. Mix well.

Macadamia Sprout Salad

2 c. alfalfa sprouts
2 c. shredded carrots
2 stalks celery, sliced
½ lb. macadamia nuts
1 c. craisins
½ c. shredded purple cabbage

 Dressing:
½ c. mayonnaise or ½ c. oil
1 tsp. salt
¼ c. sugar
Dash black pepper

Mix dressing and combine with salad.

Marinated Salad

1 can baby corn, drained and cut in half
1 red onion, chopped
1 can water chestnuts, drained
1 c. broccoli, cut in bite-size pieces
1 red pepper, thinly sliced
1 yellow pepper, thinly sliced
1 orange pepper, thinly sliced

Dressing:
1 c. water
¼ c. oil
1 T. lemon juice
¾ c. sugar
½ c. vinegar
1 tsp. salt
½ tsp. black pepper

Mix all ingredients in bowl, pour over dressing and marinate overnight.

Marinated Salad

Cauliflower
Zucchini
Carrots
Broccoli
Baby corn
Red onion
Red pepper
Green pepper
Yellow pepper
Green beans
Snow peas
½ c. oil
A little more than ½ c. vinegar
½ c. sugar
1 ½ tsp. salt
2 shakes garlic powder

Place vegetables in bowl. Add oil, vinegar, sugar, salt and garlic powder; marinate a few hours. May eliminate or add vegetables to your liking.

Marinated Salad

4 sm. zucchini, sliced
3 carrots, cut in sticks
¾ lb. fresh cut string beans, cut in half
1 pkg. mushrooms, sliced
2 red peppers, sliced
2 yellow peppers, sliced
1 sm. red onion
1 can baby corn

 Dressing:
½ c. oil
½ c. sugar
¾ c. vinegar
2 cloves garlic, minced
Pinch salt

Steam all 3 vegetables just enough to still be crunchy. Put dressing ingredients in pot; bring to a boil. Pour over all vegetables. Marinate overnight.

Marinated Vegetable Salad

1 (10-oz.) pkg. frozen cut green beans
1 (10-oz.) pkg. frozen corn
¼ c. red onion, chopped
½ c. oil
3 T. vinegar
½ tsp. salt
Dash black pepper

Cook green beans and corn according to directions on package. Drain and place in bowl. While vegetables are still warm, add rest of ingredients. Cover and chill for a few hours.

Matbucha Salad

2 big tomatoes, diced
7-8 jalapeño peppers, diced
4 cloves garlic, sliced

Sauté peppers and garlic in pot; add tomatoes. Drain juice
and simmer on stove for 5-10 minutes. While simmering, add
garlic powder, black pepper and salt.

Mesclun Salad

1 bag mesclun salad
1 red onion, diced

Dressing:
½ c oil
⅓ c. vinegar
½ tsp. crushed garlic
½ tsp. salt
2 T. brown sugar
¼ tsp. curry
1 tsp. soy sauce

Mix dressing well. Pour over mesclun and onion right
before serving.

Mixed Salad

1 red pepper, cut in strips
1 purple onion, sliced
2-4 kirbys, sliced
2 carrots, sliced
1 head cauliflower, cut in bite-size pieces
½ c. vinegar
¼ c. water
½ c oil
¾ c. sugar
3 tsp. salt

Combine everything together. Refrigerate overnight.

Mixed Green Salad

1 bag shredded lettuce
1 bag romaine lettuce
2 peppers, chopped
1 c. sliced fresh mushrooms
4-6 tomatoes, chopped

 Dressing:
3 T. red wine vinegar
2 T. Dijon mustard
1 tsp. sugar
½ tsp. salt
¾ c. oil

Combine all vegetables in bowl. Add dressing right before serving.

Mixed Vegetable Salad

1 can mixed vegetables
1 boiled potato, cubed
½ c. sliced celery
2 T. chopped green onion
⅓ c. mayonnaise
2-3 tsp. lemon juice

Combine together all ingredients in bowl. Cover and chill for 1 hour.

Mushroom Salad

1 box fresh mushrooms, sliced
1 bunch of scallions, sliced
½ c. mayonnaise
Salt & garlic powder

Place mushrooms and scallions in bowl; mix well with mayonnaise and season.

Marinated Mushrooms

1 ½ c. canned mushrooms, drained
1 c. vinegar
2 T. onions, fried
1 ½ c. water

Put vinegar, onions and water in pot; bring to a boil. Add mushrooms and cook for 10 minutes on a low flame. Refrigerate for 1 day.

Mushroom & Spinach Salad

1 bag spinach leaves
1 c. sliced fresh mushrooms

Dressing:
4 T. olive oil
2 T. balsamic vinegar
2 tsp. garlic, minced
Salt & black pepper

Combine spinach and mushrooms in bowl. Mix dressing ingredients well. Pour half of dressing on top of salad. Add more i̇ desired.

Portobello Mushroom Salad

3 lg. portobello mushrooms, sliced
2 T. oil
Salt, black pepper & paprika
1 bag euro salad
1 box cherry tomatoes, cut in half
¼ c. glazed almonds, crushed

 Dressing:
2/3 c. oil
¼ c. vinegar
¼ c. sugar
¼ c. ketchup
1 clove garlic, crushed
½ tsp. salt
¼ tsp. dry mustard
¼ tsp. paprika

Sauté mushrooms in oil, with salt, black pepper and paprika.
Combine with salad greens, tomatoes and almonds. Whisk
dressing ingredients well. Pour over salad right before serving.

Nutty Salad

1 bag romaine lettuce
1 bunch scallions, sliced
Handful toasted almonds

 Dressing:
½ c. oil
2 T. brown sugar
3 T. vinegar
½ tsp. salt

Pour dressing on salad right before serving. Garnish with
almonds.

One Bowl Salad

1 bag romaine lettuce
1 tomato, cubed
1 kirby, cubed
1 red pepper, diced
¼ c. mayonnaise
2 T. Dijonnaise
¼ c. oil
1 tsp. salt
¼ tsp. fresh garlic
Dash black pepper

Combine together all ingredients in bowl. Mix well.

Oriental Salad

1 lb. broccoli
3-5 carrots, sliced
1 pkg. snow peas
1 pkg. fresh mushrooms, sliced
1 can sliced water chestnuts, drained
1 can baby corn, drained

 Dressing:
1 c. oil
¼ c. vinegar
1 T. lemon juice
2 tsp. mustard
2 tsp. salt
¼ c. soy sauce
Dash black pepper

In individual pots, steam broccoli, carrots and snow peas for 5 minutes. Combine all vegetables in bowl. Pour dressing over salad right before serving.

3-Pepper Salad

1 carrot, shredded
1 zucchini, cubed
1 red pepper, thinly sliced
1 yellow pepper, thinly sliced
1 green pepper, thinly sliced
1 red onion, diced

Dressing:
½ c. vinegar
¼ c. oil
¼ c. sugar

Pour dressing on salad and marinate 2–3 hours.

Pepper Mix

1 (16-oz.) can peas, drained
1 (12-oz.) can white corn, drained
1 (8-oz.) can water chestnuts, drained
1 green pepper, diced
1 yellow pepper, diced
1 red pepper, diced
1 purple onion, sliced

Dressing:
¾ c. oil
1 c. water
1 c. sugar
½ tsp. black pepper
½ c. vinegar
1 T. salt

Combine vegetables in large bowl. Pour over dressing and mix well.

Pepper & Pea Salad

2 red peppers, diced
2 green peppers, diced
2 yellow peppers, diced
1 can water chestnuts, drained & sliced
1 can baby corn, drained & cut in half
1 frozen pkg. peas

Dressing:
½ c. sugar
¼ c. vinegar
1 tsp. salt
½ tsp. black pepper
⅓ c oil

Combine salad ingredients with dressing. Marinate overnight.

Hot Pepper Salad

4 peppers, cut in strips (any color)
¼ c. olive oil
Salt & black pepper

Heat oil in pan, add peppers, cover and cook until soft. Remove cover; sauté for 25 minutes on low flame. Add salt and black pepper. Serve warm.

Pickle Salad

5-6 sour pickles
4 tomatoes, cubed
1 bag frozen mixed vegetables, thawed

Mix everything in bowl. Add mayonnaise, black pepper and salt to your taste.

Pistachio Salad

1 bag euro salad
1 box grape tomatoes, sliced
1 purple onion, diced

Dressing:
½ c. mayonnaise
3 T. sugar
3 T. lemon juice
Handful pistachios
Handful craisins

Combine vegetables; pour over dressing. Top with pistachios and craisins.

Potato Salad

3-4 lg. potatoes
1 can peas & carrots, drained
4-6 gherkin pickles, diced
½ c. mayonnaise
Salt & black pepper

Cook potatoes in pot of water with peels on. While warm, peel potatoes. Let cool. Mix in remaining ingredients and chill.

Potato Salad

4 lg. potatoes, peeled
1 celery stalk, sliced
½ c. chopped green pepper
¼ c. sliced green onions
1 c. mayonnaise
1 T. Dijon mustard
1 T. horseradish
½ c. chopped fresh parsley

Cook potatoes in water until tender. Add remaining ingredients. Sprinkle with parsley. Marinate half a day in refrigerator.

Classic Potato Salad

5-6 med. potatoes, cooked, peeled and cubed
1 c. sliced celery
½ c. chopped onion
2 hard boiled eggs, chopped

Dressing:
1 c mayonnaise
2 T. vinegar
1 tsp. salt
¼ tsp. black pepper

Combine all ingredients. Mix well.

Potato & Radish Salad

1 c. mayonnaise
2 T. Dijon mustard
2 T. chopped dill
1 tsp. salt
¼ tsp. black pepper
1 ½ lbs. red potatoes, cooked & quartered
1 c. sliced radishes
½ c. chopped green onions

Combine mayonnaise, mustard, dill, salt and pepper. Pour over potatoes, radishes and onions.

Mediterranean Potato Salad

5 c. cooked small red potatoes
½ tsp. salt
¼ tsp. black pepper
3 c. thin sliced romaine lettuce
1 c. red pepper, cut in strips
1 c. yellow pepper, cut in strips
1 c. thin sliced red onion
2 T. olives

 Dressing:
1 ½ T. fresh chopped basil
1 T. fresh lemon juice
2 tsp. extra virgin olive oil
¾ tsp. sugar
¼ tsp. Dijon mustard
¼ tsp. black pepper

Cut potatoes in half; add to other salad ingredients.
Pour dressing over and mix well.

Ratatouille Salad

½ c. olive oil
1 onion, chopped
1 clove garlic, minced
2 eggplants, peeled & cubed
2 green peppers, diced
2 zucchinis, peeled & sliced
3 lg. tomatoes, cubed
Salt & black pepper
2 tsp. chopped basil

Heat oil in frying pan, add onion and garlic and sauté until soft.
Add in remaining ingredients, lower heat and cover for
30 minutes. Remove from fire and let cool. Drain vegetables
and refrigerate.

Red & Green Salad

1 bag Bodek lettuce
1 kirby, sliced
1 red pepper, sliced
1 can baby corn, drained & cut in half
1 ½ tsp. salt
¾ c. sugar
¾ c. vinegar
¾ c. oil

Combine all ingredients in bowl. Mix well.

Romaine Salad

1 bag romaine lettuce

 Dressing:
¾ c. oil
¼ c. lemon juice
Dash onion powder
½ T. crushed garlic
½ tsp. salt

Mix dressing well. Pour over lettuce right before serving.

Romaine Salad

1 bag romaine lettuce
1 c. sliced fresh mushrooms
½ box cherry tomatoes
Handful craisins

 Dressing:
½ c. vinegar
½ c. sugar
¼ c. oil
Less than ½ c. ketchup
1 clove garlic, crushed
¼ tsp. dry mustard
Dash black pepper

Mix dressing ingredients well. Pour over salad right before
serving.

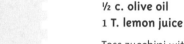

Roasted Zucchini

4 c. zucchini, sliced
½ c. olive oil
1 T. lemon juice

Toss zucchini with olive oil; roast at 350° for 15-20 minutes.
Season with salt and black pepper. Drizzle lemon juice
before serving.

Russian Salad

2 red onions, diced
1 dozen kirbys, cubed
Bunch of scallions, sliced
¼ c. vinegar
½ c. sugar
½ c. mayonnaise
½ tsp. salt
2 tsp. dill

Combine all ingredients together. Mix well.
Refrigerate overnight.

Salmon Salad

1 hard boiled egg
1 can boneless salmon
1 can mixed vegetables
1 sour pickle
1 T. vinegar
3 T. mayonnaise
Salt & black pepper

Chop egg and pickle together. In bowl, combine rest of
ingredients. Mix well.

Hot Salsa

4 Holland tomatoes, chopped
1 onion, chopped
1/3 c. jalapeño peppers
2 T. chopped cilantro
1 T. lemon juice

Combine all ingredients. Mix well and refrigerate.

Mexican Salsa

1 c. chopped tomatoes
2 T. diced avocado
2 T. cilantro, chopped
1 ½ T. chopped jalapeño pepper,
1 ½ T. lime juice
1/8 tsp. salt
½ tsp. black pepper

Mix all ingredients together and refrigerate.

Squash & Mushroom Salad

6 zucchinis, peeled & chopped
1 lg. onion, chopped
4-oz. can mushrooms, drained
8-oz. can tomato sauce
½ c. red wine
½ tsp. salt
1/8 tsp. black pepper
1 T. oil

Sauté onion in oil until tender. Add remaining ingredients.
Simmer slowly, stirring occasionally, until squash is tender,
about 20-30 minutes.

Vegetable Salads

Spanish Salad

1 bunch watercress, chopped
4 tomatoes, diced
1 cucumber, diced
1 bunch scallions, chopped
Handful stuffed olives

 Dressing:
2 T. red wine vinegar
1 tsp. paprika
½ tsp. cumin
1 garlic clove, crushed
5 T. olive oil
Salt & black pepper

Combine all ingredients in bowl. Pour dressing over salad; mix well.

Spice Salad

2 bags euro salad
1 box cherry tomatoes, cut in half
Onion & garlic croutons

 Dressing:
6 T. mayonnaise
¼ c. oil
1 T. chopped parsley
1 T. dried chives
1 T. sugar
1 tsp. lemon juice
1 tsp. dry mustard
2 tsp. crushed garlic

Combine euro salad and tomatoes in bowl. Right before serving, place onion and garlic croutons on top and pour dressing over salad.

Spinach Salad

1 bag spinach leaves
1 avocado, cubed
2 lg. tomatoes, sliced
1 can hearts of palm, drained & sliced

Dressing:
3 T. red wine vinegar
3 T. olive oil
3 T. sugar
2 tsp. dried dill
½ tsp. salt

Whisk dressing ingredients together. Pour over spinach,
tomatoes and hearts of palm right before serving. Place
avocado on top of salad.

Spinach Salad

1 bag spinach leaves
1 box fresh mushrooms, sliced
1 can water chestnuts, drained
1 red pepper, sliced
1 c. chinese noodles

Dressing:
⅓ c. lemon juice
⅓ c. vinegar
1 tsp. salt
¼ c. sugar
1 tsp. soy sauce
1 purple onion, diced
½ c. olive oil

Mix all vegetables together in bowl. Add dressing right before
serving. Garnish with chinese noodles.

Spinach Mushroom Salad

1 bag baby spinach leaves
3 c. sliced fresh mushrooms
1 purple onion, cut in rings
3 plum tomatoes, chopped

Dressing:
3 T. olive oil
3 T. Heinz red wine garlic vinegar
2 tsp. lemon juice
1 tsp. mustard
1 tsp. sugar
1 tsp. curry
½ tsp. crushed garlic
2 T. pareve imitation bacon bits

Place spinach, mushrooms, onion and tomatoes in bowl. Mix dressing well and chill at least 4 hours before adding to salad.

Baby Spinach Salad

1 pkg. baby spinach leaves
3-5 sliced fresh mushrooms
1 red onion, diced
Handful Bac-Os

Dressing:
1 c. oil
½ c. ketchup
¼ c. red wine vinegar
1 tsp. salt
1-2 T. minced onion

Mix together dressing. Add to salad ingredients and place Bac-Os on top.

Baby Spinach Salad

1 bag baby spinach leaves
1 box fresh mushrooms, sliced
1 sm. red onion, diced
Handful craisins

 Dressing:
½ c. olive oil
⅓ c. vinegar
1 tsp. salt
½ tsp. soy sauce

Mix all salad ingredients together; pour dressing over salad.

Baby Spinach Salad

2 (10-oz.) bags baby spinach leaves
1 (15-oz.) can hearts of palm, drained & sliced
1 box grape tomatoes
2 ripe avocados, diced
10 oz. sliced fresh mushrooms
½ c. slivered almonds, toasted

 Dressing:
½ c. sugar
1 tsp. salt
½ tsp. dry mustard
½ tsp. paprika
¾ c. canola oil
½ c. vinegar
½ c. ketchup
2 crushed garlic cloves

Mix all vegetables in bowl. Dressing: Mix dressing well. Pour dressing over right before serving.

Spinach Leaf Salad

2 bags baby spinach leaves
2 red peppers, diced
2 boxes fresh mushrooms, sliced
2 c. onion garlic croutons
¼ lb. pine nuts, roasted
1 tsp. salt

Dressing:
⅔ c. oil
¼ c. vinegar
¼ c. sugar
½ T. mustard

Mix spinach, peppers, mushrooms and pine nuts in bowl. Pour salt directly on salad and mix. Mix dressing well and pour over salad. Sprinkle croutons on top.

Spinach Salad

1 bag spinach leaves
1 red onion, sliced
Handful cashews
Handful craisins
9 T. olive oil
3 T. tarragon vinegar
2-4 T. sugar

Combine all ingredients in bowl and mix well.

Steamed Vegetables

1 head cauliflower
1 head broccoli
2 pkgs. carrots
1 can baby corn, drained

Dressing:
¾ c water
¾ c sugar
¾ c. vinegar
1 tsp. salt
¼ c. oil
1 ½ T. garlic powder

Steam cauliflower, broccoli and carrots; let it cool (according to directions on package). Add corn. Mix together dressing ingredients and pour over vegetables.

String Bean Salad

1 lb. fresh string beans, ends cut off
5 cloves garlic, diced
1 red pepper, diced
1 med. onion, diced
¼ c. slivered almonds
2-3 T. soy sauce

Steam string beans in one pot. Sauté onion in a different pot. Slowly add garlic and pepper to onion. Add string beans to onion pot. Mix in almonds and soy sauce and cook for another 5 minutes. Serve warm.

String Bean Salad

1 lb. fresh string beans, steamed
½ c. cubed tomatoes
½ c. cubed cucumbers
¼ c. diced green peppers
¼ c. diced onions

 Dressing:
3 T. Dijon mustard
1 T. balsamic vinegar

Pour dressing over vegetables. Chill in refrigerator 1-2 hours before serving.

String Bean Salad

1 lb. string beans, ends cut off
1 clove garlic, chopped
2 T. red wine vinegar
¼ c. olive oil
Salt & black pepper

Bring pot of salted water to boil, add string beans and cook for 7 minutes. Remove from flame and let cool. Mix in rest of ingredients to string beans.

Sugar Snap Pea Salad

1 lb. sugar snap peas, trimmed
12 medium radishes, diced
⅓ c. chopped leek
2 T. sliced fresh basil

 Dressing:
2 T. olive oil
1 T. red wine vinegar
½ tsp. sugar
½ tsp. salt
¼ tsp. black pepper

Combine dressing ingredients in bowl. Refrigerate until ready to serve. Fill large bowl with water and ice cubes; set aside. Bring pot of salted water to boil. Add sugar snap peas; cook for

3 minutes. Drain. Rinse with cold water. Transfer to ice water for 10 minutes. Drain and transfer to serving bowl. Mix in radishes, leek and basil. Toss with refrigerated dressing.

Sushi Salad

1 c. brown rice
2 c. water
Pinch of salt
2 sheets nori seaweed
2 T. rice vinegar
2 tsp. prepared wasabi (Japanese horseradish)
¾ c. shredded carrots
¾ c. shredded radishes
½ c. chopped broccoli
1 avocado, cut into ½-inch cubes
3 T. toasted sesame seed
Pickled ginger for garnish (opt.)

Cook rice in water and salt according to your usual method. Turn cooked rice out into a large bowl or platter, spreading it out to cool to warm or room temperature. Meanwhile, if the nori seaweed is not already toasted, toast the sheets one at a time by holding with two hands on opposite sides and carefully moving the sheet back and forth over an open gas range flame set at low temperature for about 1-2 minutes. Tear the toasted nori sheets into small, bite-sized pieces; set aside on a paper towel or small, dry dish.

NOTE: Be sure that your hands are perfectly dry when handling the nori or the pieces may stick to each other. Blend together vinegar and prepared wasabi; set aside. When rice has reached the cooler temperature, gently stir in vinegar-wasabi mixture, slightly warm or at room temperature, and garnish with hand-rolled rosettes of pickled ginger. Makes 4-6 servings.

Supreme Salad

1 bag salad mix
3 scallions, sliced
2 c. fresh sliced mushrooms
2 avocados, diced
1 c. slivered almonds
1 c. dried cranberries
1/3 c. olive oil
1/4 c. vinegar
Salt & black pepper to taste

Combine all ingredients in bowL

Sweet & Sour Salad

1 bag romaine lettuce
6 radishes, thinly sliced
1/2 purple onion, minced
1/2 yellow pepper, diced
1/2 red pepper, diced
1/3 c. cooked chickpeas
2 oranges, sliced
1 c. grape tomatoes, halved
1/2 c. fresh basil

Dressing:
4 T. olive oil
4 T. lemon juice
1 tsp. cumin
1 tsp. crushed garlic
1 tsp. white sugar
1/4 tsp. paprika
1/8 tsp. cayenne pepper

Combine all of the salad ingredients in large bowl. Mix together dressing ingredients. Chill dressing at least 2 hours. Add to salad before serving.

Taco Salad

1 bag red leaf lettuce
¼ c. shredded purple cabbage
3 avocados, cubed
½ can black olives
1 bag barbeque tacos, crushed

 Dressing:
  ¼ c. salsa
  ⅓ c. ketchup
  1 c. mayonnaise

Combine all vegetables in bowl. Pour dressing over salad;
sprinkle crushed tacos on top.

Terra Chip Salad

½ c. red pepper, cut in strips
½ c. yellow pepper, cut in strips
1 avocado, cubed
1 c. spinach leaves
1 bag romaine lettuce
6 oz. slivered almonds
4 oz. pignoli nuts
1 bag terra chips

 Dressing:
  ⅓ c. oil
  ⅓ c. red wine vinegar
  ¼ c. sugar
  3 T. ketchup
  2 T. grated onion

Combine all vegetables in bowl. Mix dressing well. Pour
dressing over salad right before serving and place crushed
chips on top.

Vegetable Salads

Tomato & Avocado Salad

1 box red cherry tomatoes, cut in half
1 ripe avocado, cubed
1 T. chopped fresh cilantro leaves
2 tsp. fresh lime juice
⅛ tsp. salt

Combine all ingredients. Mix well.

Tomato & Basil Salad

1 box cherry or grape tomatoes
1 onion, diced
1 tsp. crushed garlic
Handful fresh basil
Dash olive oil
Salt & pepper to taste
Fresh, hot bread

Dice finely tomatoes, onion and garlic. Sprinkle chopped basil on vegetables. Add dash of olive oil, salt and black pepper to taste. Mix well. Serve over fresh, hot bread.

Tomato & Chickpea Salad

2-3 tomatoes, cubed
1 can chickpeas, drained
½ c. sliced olives
½ red onion, diced

Dressing:
½ c. sugar
½ c. vinegar
1 ½ tsp. salt
¼ c oil
¼ c. olive oil
½ tsp. black pepper
Dash garlic powder

Combine vegetables and dressing together. Mix well.

Tomato & Corn Salad

4 corn on the cob, corn sliced off
4 tomatoes, cubed
2 T. sugar
3 T. olive oil
Salt & black pepper

Bring pot of water to boil, add corn and sugar and boil for 1
minute. Drain corn; pat dry. Mix tomatoes with corn. Season
with salt and black pepper and drizzle with olive oil.

Tomato Salad with Garlic

2 ripe tomatoes, cut in chunks
½ box red & yellow cherry tomatoes, cut in half
½ c. sliced black olives
1 T. balsamic vinegar
2 T. olive oil
2 garlic cloves, thinly sliced
3 oregano leaves
Salt & black pepper

Heat oil in pan over medium heat; add garlic until golden
brown. Remove from heat, let cool and add oregano. Place
tomatoes in bowl. Season with salt and black pepper. Pour
garlic mixture on tomatoes. Add vinegar and olives. Mix well.

Tomato Olive Salad

4 tomatoes, sliced
½ c. sliced olives
1 med. onion, cut in rings
1 T. vinegar
¼ c. oil
¼ tsp. salt

Combine all ingredients. Marinate overnight.

Tomato & Olive Salad

5 plum tomatoes, diced
1 red onion, cut in thin circles
½ c. sliced black olives
¼ c. chopped fresh basil

Dressing:
¼ c. olive oil
1 tsp. red wine vinegar
Salt & black pepper

Mix together tomatoes, onion, olives and basil. Whisk together dressing and pour over vegetables.

Tomato & Olive Salad

3 Holland tomatoes, cubed
1 c. stuffed olives
2 scallions, diced
3 garlic cloves, crushed
⅓ c. olive oil
Salt & black pepper

Combine first four ingredients; mix in oil and spices.

Tomato Olive Relish

2 lg. tomatoes, chopped
½ c. chopped green olives
2 T. chopped fresh parsley
1 tsp. olive oil
¼ tsp. salt
¼ tsp. black pepper
1 clove garlic, minced

Mix all ingredients together.

Tomato Salad

6-8 sm. tomatoes, cut in circles
2 T. olive oil
2 T. sugar
1 T. vinegar
1 T. chives
½ tsp. black pepper
½ tsp. salt

Mix together all ingredients. Marinate for 1 hour.

Tomato Salad

6 plum tomatoes, sliced
6 T. oil
2 T. vinegar
1 T. parsley
½ tsp. garlic
½ tsp. basil
½ tsp. salt
Dash black pepper

Combine all ingredients. Marinate 1-2 days.

Tomato Salad

4 ripe tomatoes, diced
1 scallion, diced
1 fresh garlic, minced
2-4 T. olive oil
Salt & black pepper to taste

Mix all ingredients together.

Tomato Salsa

1 hot chili pepper
4 tomatoes, seeded & chopped
2 c. corn
5 scallions, chopped
1 T. chopped fresh parsley
2 T. chopped cilantro
2 T. lemon juice
3 T. olive oil
1 tsp. salt

Cut chili very finely, add rest of ingredients and mix well.

Tomato & Zucchini Salad

3-4 zucchini
2 tomatoes
1 scallion, sliced

 Dressing:
Pinch black pepper
1 small onion, diced
¼ tsp. garlic powder
¼ tsp. salt
2 T. oil

Wash zucchinis well; cube with peels on. Place zucchinis in pot of salted water, boil for a few minutes and drain. Add tomatoes and scallion and mix with dressing.

Tortilla Salad

1 bag lettuce
1 box cherry tomatoes, cut in half
2 avocados, cubed
1 red pepper, finely diced
1 yellow pepper, finely diced
1 green pepper, finely diced
1 red onion, sliced
½ pkg. tortilla chips, crushed
1 c. salsa
½ c. mayonnaise

Combine all vegetables in bowl. Pour dressing over salad. Sprinkle chips on top.

Tuna Salad with a Twist

¾ c. mayonnaise
3 T. lime juice
½ tsp. grated lime peel
2 cans tuna, flaked
1 med. red pepper, cubed
1 med. cucumber, chopped
⅓ c. sliced green onions

Combine all ingredients in one bowl. Mix well. Cover and chill until serving.

Tuna Trifle Salad

½ bag lettuce
4 carrots, grated
Bunch of scallions
Radishes
Red pepper
Kirby
Celery
2 cans tuna
Mayonnnaise as desired
1 bag shredded purple cabbage
Alfalfa sprouts

Dressing:
½ - ¾ c. mayonnaise
2 T. honey
3 shakes of garlic powder

Place lettuce on bottom of trifle bowl and then carrots; layer on top scallions, radishes, red pepper, kirby and celery. Dice, slice and use any variation for more layers. Add tuna, drained and chopped finely with mayonnaise. Place purple cabbage over tuna. Glaze with dressing. Garnish with alfalfa sprouts on top.

Vegetables in Wine

1 c. Chinese peas, trimmed
4 c. cauliflower, cut up
½ c. thinly sliced carrots
½ c. thinly sliced celery
1 T. minced onion
2 T. margarine
1 chicken bouillon cube
¾ c. white wine
Salt & pepper to taste
Parsley

Melt butter or margarine in large pot. Add vegetables to pot. In bowl, combine chicken cube with wine and spices. Pour over vegetables. Cook for 10 minutes on high flame. Sprinkle with cut-up parsley.

Warm Pita Salad

2 T. olive oil
1 red onion, diced
2 c. pita bread, diced
2 tomatoes, diced
1 cucumber, diced
¼ c. chopped parsley
3 T. lemon juice
½ tsp. salt
Black pepper to taste
1 bag romaine lettuce

Heat oil in frying pan. Add onion and sauté for a few minutes; add bread and continue sautéing for another 5 minutes until onion is tender. Transfer to bowl; add rest of ingredients in order except for lettuce and stir gently. Arrange lettuce on individual plates and spoon salad onto lettuce. Serve immediately.

Salads with
Fruit

Apple Salad

2 med. green apples, diced
1 c. sliced strawberries
2 kiwis, diced
1 sm. orange, squeezed
Cinnamon flatbreads

 Dressing:
2 T. brown sugar
2 T. apple or orange jam
1 tsp. lemon juice

Combine salad ingredients. Mix salad with dressing. Serve with cinnamon flatbreads.

Asparagus Salad

1 bag romaine lettuce
8 oz. asparagus, trimmed & cut in half
2 ripe tomatoes, cut in wedges
2 oranges

 Dressing:
2 T. olive oil
½ tsp. sherry vinegar
Salt & black pepper

Cook asparagus in boiling salted water. Drain and set aside. Grate the rind from one orange. Cut both oranges in cubes. Squeeze juice from membrane and put aside. Combine asparagus, tomatoes, oranges and lettuce in bowl. Mix dressing ingredients with reserved juice and rind. Pour dressing over salad right before serving.

Avocado Salad

1 bag romaine lettuce
1 red onion, diced
2 avocados, cubed
2 cans mandarin oranges, drained
Handful toasted slivered almonds

 Dressing:
½ c. oil
⅓ c. vinegar
½ c. sugar
2 tsp. dried mustard
2 tsp. salt
Handful poppy seeds

Combine together all ingredients, mixing very well.

Pecan Avocado Salad

1 can mandarin oranges
½ c. sliced purple onion
⅓ c. pecans
⅛ tsp. black pepper
4 c. salad greens
1 ripe avocado, sliced
¼ c. Italian dressing

Combine together all ingredients. Pour Italian dressing over salad right before serving.

Caramelized Almond Salad

1 bag salad mix
1 can mandarin oranges, drained
1 c. caramelized almonds
1 red onion, diced
2 T. vinegar
2 T. sugar
2 T. oil
½ tsp. salt
¼ tsp. black pepper

Combine all ingredients in bowl. Mix well.

Carrot Salad

6 lg. carrots, shredded
¼ c. raisins
1 can crushed pineapple, slightly drained
¼ c. sunflower seeds
½ tsp. lemon juice
⅛ c. mayonnaise
½ c. ground coconut

Mix together all ingredients 1 day in advance of serving.
Refrigerate.

Cabbage Salad

1 bag green cabbage, shredded
1 sm. can mandarin oranges, drained
1 scallion, sliced
¼ c. chopped almonds
1 T. sesame seeds

 Dressing:
6 T. vinegar
¼ c. oil
¼ c. sugar

Combine salad ingredients. Whisk together dressing
ingredients. Pour over salad.

Purple Cabbage Salad

1 (10-oz.) bag shredded purple cabbage
1 bag Bodek lettuce
3 scallions, sliced
½ c. sunflower seeds
⅓ c. slivered almonds
1 c. mandarin oranges, drained
2 c. thin chow mein noodles

 Dressing:
½ c. oil
¼ c. brown sugar
1 tsp. salt
⅜ c. vinegar

Combine vegetables and fruit. Whisk together dressing
ingredients. Pour over vegetables and fruit and mix well.

Red Cabbage & Apple Salad

1 (10-oz.) bag shredded red cabbage
2 apples, diced

 Dressing:
1 c. mayonnaise
Juice of 1 lemon
4 T. sugar
1 tsp. cinnamon

Mix together cabbage and apples. Pour dressing over and chill.

Colorful Salad

2 bags euro salad
1 can mandarin oranges
2 mangos, diced
1 pkg. snow peas
1 handful cashews

 Dressing:
½ clove garlic
½ tsp. mustard
¼ c. ketchup
¼ c. vinegar
¼ c. oil
¼ c. sugar
½ tsp. salt
½ tsp. paprika

Blend dressing ingredients in food processor. Pour dressing over salad right before serving.

Craisin Salad

1 bag euro salad
¾ c. craisins
1 sm. purple onion, diced

 Dressing:
½ c. mayonnaise
1 T. mustard
1 box onion garlic croutons

Combine all ingredients in bowl. Pour croutons on salad before serving.

Cranberry Salad

1 bag coleslaw
½ c. cranberries
2 handfuls chow mein noodles
A little less than ¼ c. vinegar
¼ c. oil
1 tsp. salt
1 tsp. black pepper
2 tsp. sugar

Combine together ingredients. Add chow mein noodles before serving.

Crunch Salad

½ bag shredded lettuce
½ bag shredded red cabbage
2 stalks celery, sliced
1 can mandarin oranges, drained
Handful slivered almonds

Dressing:
¼ c. oil
2 T. vinegar
2 T. brown sugar
Salt & black pepper

Combine all ingredients in bowl. Pour dressing over salad ½ hour before serving.

Didi's Salad

1 bag euro salad
1 can mandarin oranges, drained
1 red onion, thinly sliced
Handful craisins
Handful honeyed almonds

Dressing:
2 T. red wine vinegar
2 T. lemon juice
¼ c. olive oil
1 tsp. dry mustard
2 T. sugar
½ tsp. salt
½ tsp. garlic powder

Mix dressing well. Pour over salad. Add almonds right before serving.

Euro Salad

1 bag euro salad
1 mango, cubed
1 box fresh strawberries, sliced
¾ c. slivered almonds
Handful craisins & sunflower seeds

Dressing:
⅛ tsp. vinegar
½ tsp. salt
3 oz. oil
⅛ c. sugar

Combine dressing ingredients; pour over euro salad, mango, strawberries and almonds right before serving. Sprinkle on top craisins and sunflower seeds.

Exotic Salad

1 bag euro salad
2 med. grapefruits, peeled & cubed
3 oranges, peeled & cubed
1 ripe avocado, cubed
¼ c. toasted slivered almonds

 Dressing:
½ c. oil
⅓ c. sugar
3 T. vinegar
2 tsp. poppy seed
1 tsp. grated onion
½ tsp. dry mustard
½ tsp. salt

Combine all ingredients in bowl. Pour dressing over salad
before serving.

Jamaican Salad

4 c. salad greens
2 c. fresh pineapple chunks
1 c. chopped papaya

 Dressing:
2 tsp. dried thyme
2 T. fresh lime juice
1 T. olive oil
1 T. fresh minced ginger
2 tsp. brown sugar
½ tsp. salt
½ tsp. allspice
½ tsp. cinnamon
¼ tsp. black pepper
1 clove garlic, minced

Combine salad ingredients in bowl. Combine all dressing
ingredients in food processor until smooth. Pour 2 tablespoons
of dressing over salad. Store rest of dressing in refrigerator.
(Add more if desired).

Mango Salsa

2 c. plum tomatoes, diced
1 ½ c. diced mango
½ c. diced red onion
½ c. chopped cilantro
2 T. lime juice
1 T. cider vinegar
1 tsp. sugar
½ tsp. salt
½ tsp. black pepper
2 cloves garlic, minced

Combine together all ingredients. Chill before serving.

Mango Salsa

2 ripe mangoes, peeled & diced
2 red peppers, cut in thin strips
1 red onion, finely chopped
½ c. chopped cilantro leaves
1-2 garlic cloves, minced
1 jalapeño chili, finely chopped
¼ c. fresh orange juice
Juice of 3 limes

Combine all ingredients in bowl; gently mix together.
Cover and refrigerate. Will keep good for 2-3 days.

Mango Strawberry Salad

1 bag euro salad
¾ c. craisins
¾ c. glazed almonds
2 mangos, diced
1 box fresh strawberries, sliced

Dressing:
¼ c. oil
¼ c. sugar
¼ c. vinegar

Combine all salad ingredients in large bowl. Whisk together
dressing and pour over salad.

Orange Salad

2 cans mandarin oranges, drained
1 bag shredded lettuce
1 bag romaine lettuce
1 cucumber, chopped
½ pkg. slivered almonds

Dressing:
3 T. mayonnaise
4 T. olive oil
3 tsp. lemon juice
Dash sugar, black pepper & garlic powder

Combine salad ingredients. Whisk together dressing.
Pour on top.

Peach & Pink Grapefruit Salad

2 ½ c. diced peaches
2 lg. pink grapefruits, peeled & cubed
⅓ c. small mint leaves
¼ tsp. salt
¼ tsp. black pepper

Dressing:
⅓ c. rice vinegar
2 T. brown sugar
½ c. chopped red onion

Place vinegar and sugar in pot and bring to boil. Place onion
in large bowl and pour vinegar mixture over it; let cool. When
cooled, add rest of ingredients, mixing slowly.

Pineapple Salad

2 c. diced apples
1 c. chunk pineapple
1 c. chopped celery
⅔ c. chopped walnuts

 Dressing:
¼ c. mayonnaise
1 T. sugar
½ tsp. lemon juice
¼ tsp. salt

Combine salad ingredients. Pour dressing on top. Mix well.

Raspberry & Watermelon Salad

4-6 c. seeded & cubed watermelon
1 box fresh raspberries
¼ c. sugar
Juice of 1 lemon

Combine all ingredients in bowl. Let stand for 30 minutes, mixing occasionally, until sugar is dissolved. Serve chilled.

Sardine Salad

2 cans sardines, skinless & boneless
3 hard-boiled eggs
1 small onion, grated
1 medium apple, grated
Juice of ½ lemon
2 T. sugar
½ tsp. salt
Crackers

Mash sardines and eggs well. Combine rest of ingredients. Serve on crackers.

Seven Layer Salad

1 bag shredded red cabbage
1 bag shredded lettuce
1 tomato, cubed
1 c. sliced mushrooms
1 can mandarin oranges, drained
¼ c. sunflower seeds

Dressing:
6 T. vinegar
4 T. brown sugar
1 tsp. salt
⅓ c. oil

Layer vegetables and fruit in a glass trifle bowl in the order
listed. Whisk dressing ingredients well. Pour on top of salad
before serving.

Spinach Salad with Raspberry Vinaigrette

1 lb. fresh spinach leaves
2 big onions, chopped
2 c. sliced fresh strawberries

Dressing:
½ c. raspberry vinegar
½ c. olive oil
¼ c. sugar
½ tsp. salt

Mix dressing and chill. Place spinach and onions in bowl. Top
with strawberries; drizzle dressing on top of salad right before
serving.

Salads with Fruit

Terra Stix Salad

1 bag muscular salad mix
1 red onion, sliced
Handful craisins
1 can mandarin oranges, drained
1 handful pine nuts
1 cucumber, sliced
½ bag terra stix, or as much as desired

Dressing:
½ c. oil
4 T. red wine vinegar
2 tsp. minced garlic
Dash salt & black pepper
2 T. Dijon mustard
3 T. sugar
2 T. balsamic vinegar

Combine dressing ingredients in food processor.
Pour dressing over salad. Add terra stix on salad just
before serving.

Tropical Salad

1 bag euro salad
1 box strawberries, sliced
3 kiwis, sliced
1 mango, cubed
Handful craisins
Handful honey-glazed almonds

Dressing:
2 wild berry zinger tea bags
½ c. water
¼ c. oil
¼ c. vinegar
¼ c. sugar
¾ tsp. salt

Place tea bags in water. Remove tea bags. Combine tea,
oil, vinegar, sugar and salt. Mix well. Pour dressing over euro
salad, strawberries, kiwis and mango. Garnish with craisins
and almonds.

2-Tone Salad

1 bunch broccoli, cut in bite-size pieces
1 bunch cauliflower, cut in bite-size pieces
1 red onion, diced
Handful dark raisins
Handful salted cashews

Dressing:
 1 c. mayonnaise
 ½ c. sugar
 ¼ c vinegar
 1 T. wine

Combine salad ingredients. Whisk together dressing;
pour on top.

Waldorf Salad

3 c. diced apples
½ c. chopped celery
½ c. halved & seeded red grapes
½ c. chopped walnuts

Dressing:
 ½ c. mayonnaise
 1 T. sugar
 ½ tsp. lemon juice

Combine dressing into fruit mixture and chill in refrigerator
until serving.

Salads with Fruit

Pasta
Salads

Angel Hair Pasta
& Purple Cabbage

½ box angel hair pasta
1 bunch scallions, sliced
1 bag shredded purple cabbage
2 dashes salt
1 dash black pepper
¼ c. toasted sesame seed
½ c. vinegar
½ c. sugar
¼ c. oil

Cook pasta in boiling water. Drain. Combine with rest of
ingredients. Let marinate in refrigerator for a few hours.

Angel Hair Pasta
with Vegetables

1 box angel hair pasta
Oil
3 bunches scallions (only green part)
½ lg. garlic clove, diced
8 plum tomatoes, diced

Boil and drain pasta. Heat oil in large pot; sauté scallions, garlic
and tomatoes until soft. Mix vegetables with pasta.

Caterpillar Salad

1 box caterpillar noodles, cooked & drained
1 box cherry tomatoes, cut in half
4 scallions, chopped
1 tsp. polaner garlic
½ tsp. crushed basil
⅓ c. olive oil
1 tsp. salt
½ tsp. black pepper
1 can baby corn, drained

Combine all ingredients in large bowl. Mix well.

Creamy Italian Pasta Salad

1 box spiral macaroni, cooked & drained
1 c. cherry tomatoes
½ c. chopped green pepper
½ c. sliced green or black olives

 Dressing:
1 c. mayonnaise
2 T. red wine vinegar
1 clove garlic, minced
1 tsp. dried basil
1 tsp. salt
¼ tsp. black pepper

Combine dressing ingredients. Pour over remaining ingredients.

Garlic Pasta

1 box angel hair pasta, cooked & drained
6 cloves garlic, chopped
2 tsp. olive oil
¼ c. parsley flakes
Salt to taste

Sauté garlic in oil; add in parsley flakes and salt. Add mixture to pasta. Mix well.

Pasta Salads

Linguini Salad

1 box linguini
1 bag shredded purple cabbage
1 bunch scallions, very thinly sliced
1 c. roasted slivered almonds
2 handfuls craisins

Dressing:
⅓ c. oil
½ c. vinegar
½ c. sugar
1 tsp. salt

Cook linguini according to directions on box. Drain and cool. Combine all ingredients in a large bowl. Mix dressing well and pour over salad.

Linguini Salad

1 lb. linguini noodles
2 T. chopped scallions
2 T. parsley
¼ tsp. basil

Dressing:
1 c. Italian dressing
1 c. mayonnaise

Cook spaghetti according to package. When cooled, mix in dressing.

Garlic Linguini Salad

1 box linguini, cooked & drained
1 c. olive oil
¼ c. red wine vinegar
1 tsp. crushed garlic
Bunch scallions
1 ½ tsp. salt
1 tsp. black pepper
¾ c. whipped topping, unwhipped

Put ingredients except topping into food processor; use chop blade for 30 seconds. Slowly add topping while machine is on. Add noodles and mix well.

Tomato Linguini Salad

1 box linguini noodles, cooked & drained
3 plum tomatoes, cubed
1 bunch scallions, sliced

 Dressing:
    1/3 c. olive oil
    2 tsp. salt
    1/2 tsp. red pepper spice
    1 tsp. garlic

Combine linguine, tomatoes and scallions in bowl.
Add dressing when noodles are still warm. Mix well.

Oriental Salad

2 c. orzo, cooked & drained
2 onions, chopped
1/2 lb. mushrooms, sliced
1 c. water chestnuts
1 clove garlic, minced
1 green pepper, diced
1 c. bamboo shoots
1/2 can baby corn, drained

 Sauce:
    3 oz. soy sauce
    2 tsp. sugar
    1 oz. water
    1 tsp. cornstarch

Boil orzo and drain. Sauté garlic in oil. Add vegetables and
sauté for 5 minutes. Pour sauce over vegetables and bring to a
boil. Remove from pot and pour over orzo.

Pasta Salads

Orzo Salad

1 lb. orzo
½ c. craisins
½ c. pine nuts
½ c. oil
Japanese mix (baby carrots, broccoli, mushrooms)
1 can mandarin oranges, drained
4 T. onion soup mix

Cook orzo; add rest of ingredients in 9 x 13-inch pan. Cover.
Bake for 1 hour at 350°.

Spicy Broccoli Orzo Salad

8 oz. orzo
2 ½ c. fresh broccoli, cut in bite-size pieces
2 tomatoes, diced
3 scallions, sliced
3 T. parsley

Dressing:
1 T. olive oil
1 T. red wine vinegar
1 tsp. salt
1 tsp. black pepper
1 tsp. garlic powder

Cook orzo according to directions. Add in remaining
ingredients and mix well.

Pasta Primavera

1 lb. penne noodles
4 c. broccoli florets
2 peppers, seeded & chopped
2 med. zucchini, thinly sliced
2 yellow squash, thinly sliced
3 cloves garlic, minced
2 tomatoes, peeled, seeded & diced
½ c. fresh peas
¾ c. fresh parsley
4 T. fresh basil leaves
3 T. chicken bouillon

Spray a pan with cooking spray. Add broccoli, peppers, zucchini, squash and garlic to pan. Sauté for 5 minutes. Add tomatoes and peas and sauté for 2 minutes. Place parsley, basil and chicken bouillon in food processor until finely chopped. Cook pasta according to package directions and drain. Combine all ingredients in one bowl.

Pasta with Sun-dried Tomatoes

1 box spiral noodles
Handful sun-dried tomatoes
1 ctn. spinach dip (ready made)
Salt & black pepper to taste

Cook and drain pasta according to box. Mix pasta with remaining ingredients.

Pasta Salads

Penne Salad

1 box penne pasta
½ box grape tomatoes
1 tsp. crushed red hot pepper
2 tsp. salt
1 T. basil
¾ c. oil
1 T. crushed garlic
1 tsp. black pepper

Cook noodles according to package and drain. Combine rest of ingredients with noodles. Mix well.

Sesame Noodle Salad

16 oz. linguini
1 red pepper, diced
1 green pepper, diced
Bunch scallions, diced
⅓ c. toasted sesame seeds

Dressing:
4-6 T. brown sugar
3-5 T. sesame oil
¼ - ⅓ c. soy sauce
¼ tsp. garlic powder
¼ tsp. salt
Dash black pepper

Cook and drain pasta. Pour dressing ingredients over pasta. Mix in pepper, sesame seeds and scallions.

Spaghetti Salad

1 box spaghetti, cooked & drained
1 red pepper, diced
1 green pepper, diced
1 c. toasted sesame seeds

Dressing:
½ c. oil
½ c. mayonnaise
½ c. soy sauce
¼ c. sugar
½ tsp. garlic powder

Mix together dressing ingredients. Pour over salad.

Spiral Salad

1 box spiral pasta
1 red pepper, diced
1 green pepper, diced
1 yellow pepper, diced
1 can black olives, sliced
1 can corn
1 can peas

Dressing:
1 c. olive oil
1 box spinach, thawed
2 cloves garlic
2 tsp. salt
2 T. basil

Boil pasta and drain. Mix in remaining ingredients. Place all dressing ingredients in blender. Pour over noodles.

Tri-color Pasta

1 box tri-colored pasta, cooked & drained

Dressing:
½ c. sugar
½ c. vinegar
⅔ c. oil
4 tsp. salt
1 bunch scallions, sliced

Whisk dressing ingredients well. Pour over noodles just before serving.

Tri-color Salad

1 box tri-color noodles
½ bunch scallions, diced
¼ green pepper, chopped
2 sour pickles, chopped
8 T. sugar
3 ½ T. vinegar
¾ c. warm water
2 T. mayonnaise

Boil noodles in salted water and drain. Combine scallions, pepper and pickles with sugar, vinegar and water. Mix well. Add pasta and mayonnaise to vegetables. Refrigerate before serving.

Dairy
Salads

Broccoli with Sauce

1 bunch fresh broccoli
2 c. salted water

Sauce:
1 c. sour cream
3 T. finely chopped onion
½ tsp. celery seed
¼ tsp. salt
1 tsp. sugar
2 tsp. vinegar
1 tsp. horseradish

Boil broccoli in salted water, covered, 10-12 minutes. If serving broccoli hot, pour sauce over right away and serve. If serving cold, chill broccoli first, then pour over sauce.

Creamy Milchig Salad

1 bag romaine lettuce
½ box fresh mushrooms, sliced
1 box cherry tomatoes
1 red onion, sliced in thin rings
Croutons

Combine ingredients in large bowl.

Dressing:
2 ½ slices Muenster cheese
3 T. cottage cheese
²/₃ c. oil
2 cloves garlic
¼ c. vinegar
2 tsp. sugar
1 tsp. salt

Combine all dressing ingredients in blender. Pour dressing over salad ingredients right before serving. Add croutons on top.

Cottage Cheese Salad

1 T. sunflower seeds
1 T. sesame seeds
1 c. lowfat cottage cheese
2 celery stalks, diced
1 carrot, shredded
½ cucumber, diced
½ red pepper, diced
1 T. parsley, chopped
Lettuce

Place sunflower seeds and sesame seeds in oven at 350° for 10 minutes. In bowl, combine all other ingredients, including the seeds. Serve on bed of lettuce.

Crunchy Spring Salad

1 bunch radishes
2 cucumbers
1 bunch scallions
2 tomatoes
2 peppers (any color)
2 carrots
½ c. cottage cheese
½ c. sour cream
Lettuce

Cut, slice or dice vegetables. Combine with cottage cheese and sour cream. Serve on bed of lettuce.

Dairy Salad

1 bag romaine lettuce
1 tomato, sliced
1 c. croutons

Dressing:
½ c. cottage cheese
2 T. plain yogurt
1 T. wine vinegar
1 T. lemon juice
1 T. oil
l egg
1 clove garlic
¼ c. Parmesan cheese
¼ tsp. black pepper

Combine dressing ingredients in blender. Arrange lettuce, tomatoes and croutons on individual plates. Drizzle with dressing.

Delightful Fruit Salad

1 can light fruit cocktail
1 can pineapple tidbits
1 box fresh strawberries, diced
1 can mandarin oranges
1 banana, sliced
1 c. light cottage cheese
1 small carton whipped topping

In large bowl, combine together ingredients except for whipped topping. Chill for 30 minutes; place in individual bowls. Top with whipped topping and serve.

Greek Goddess Salad

1 bag romaine lettuce
1 green pepper, thinly sliced
2 tomatoes, cut in wedges
½ c. sliced olives

Dressing:
¼ c. shredded feta cheese
2 ½ T. lemon juice
2 tsp. olive oil
¼ tsp. dried oregano
¼ tsp. black pepper

Combine salad ingredients. Pour dressing ingredients over salad. Add shredded feta cheese on top.

Green Beans & Cheese

1 lb. green beans, washed & cut
¼ c. olive oil
1 clove garlic, minced
2 T. chopped onion
½ c. diced red pepper
¼ c. boiling water
½ tsp. salt
1 tsp. dried basil leaves
⅓ c. grated Parmesan cheese

Heat oil in large frying pan. Sauté garlic, onion and red pepper for 2 minutes. Add water, salt, basil and green beans. Cook 8-10 minutes. Place in serving dish. Sprinkle with Parmesan cheese. Serve right away.

Dairy Salads

Leafy Salad

1 bag leafy lettuce
1 bunch radishes
2-3 hard-boiled eggs, sliced

Dressing:
1 c. chopped parsley
½ c. olive oil
2 T. lemon juice
½ tsp. sugar
½ c. plain yogurt
¼ - ½ tsp. salt

Combine lettuce, radishes and eggs in bowl. Whisk together dressing and pour over salad.

Pasta with Cheese

3 c. spiral noodles
5 oz. green beans, trimmed & cut
1 potato, diced
½ box grape tomatoes
2 scallions, chopped
1 c. shredded Parmesan cheese
6 black olives, sliced

Dressing:
6 T. olive oil
1 T. balsamic vinegar
1 T. chopped parsley
Salt & black pepper

Boil pasta in salted water 8-10 minutes, until tender. Drain and rinse under cold water. Cook green beans and potato until tender. Combine dressing ingredients with pasta and vegetables. Cover and chill for 30 minutes. Place cheese on top.

Summer Salad

5 carrots, shredded
4 celery stalks, diced
3 kirbys, diced
1 red pepper, diced
1 green pepper, diced
3 tomatoes, chopped
1 c. shredded Monterey Jack cheese
7-oz. pkg. dry Italian style mix

Dressing:
⅛ c. balsamic vinegar
⅛ c. white wine vinegar

Combine all ingredients in bowl. Mix dressing ingredients
together and drizzle over salad. Chill for 30 minutes.

Tuna Salad Supreme

1 bag lettuce
2 cans tuna, shredded
1 red onion, sliced
Chinese noodles

Dressing:
½ c. mayonnaise
2 tsp. sugar
¾ c. sour cream

Combine lettuce, tuna and onion. Mix in dressing.
Garnish with chinese noodles.

Salads with Meats

Salads with Meats

Chicken & Asparagus

2 lbs. asparagus
1 T. sesame oil
½ tsp. seasoned salt
¼ c. chicken broth
2 T. soy sauce
2 c. cooked chicken, cut in bite-size pieces
2 T. cider vinegar
Salt & black pepper

Heat oil in frying pan, cut up asparagus and stir-fry for 2 minutes. Add spices. Stir for 1 minute; pour in broth and soy sauce. Cover and cook for 1–2 minutes. Remove from heat, add chicken and mix. Refrigerate until serving; before serving, mix in vinegar.

Chicken & Asparagus

1 lb. chicken cutlets, cut in bite-size pieces
1 can asparagus
½ c. mayonnaise
1 bottle Italian dressing
3 T. sugar

Marinate chicken in half of a bottle of Italian dressing. Grill or broil until done. Combine chicken with asparagus; mix with mayonnaise and rest of Italian dressing and sugar.

Chef Salad

1 bag euro salad
1 bag romaine lettuce
Onion garlic croutons
Turkey breast & pastrami, shredded

Dressing:
¼ c. honey
¼ c. sugar
¼ c. red wine vinegar
1 tsp. Dijon mustard
¾ c. oil
Salt & black pepper

Combine euro salad and lettuce with turkey and pastrami.
Pour dressing ingredients over salad just before serving. Add
croutons on top.

Chinese Salad

1 lb. chicken cutlets, cut in bite-size pieces
Soy sauce

Dip chicken in soy sauce. Bake at 350° for 7-10 minutes on
each side.

1 bag romaine lettuce
1 red pepper, cut in strips
Handful snow peas
1 can baby corn, drained
2 kirbys, sliced
Chinese noodles

Dressing:
¼ c. sugar
¼ c. oil
¼ c. white vinegar
⅛ c. soy sauce
2 tsp. polaner garlic

Combine vegetables and chicken. Pour dressing over right
before serving. Garnish with chinese noodles.

Chinese Chicken Salad

2 chicken cutlets
2 tsp. light soy sauce
1 tsp. sesame oil
1 tsp. sesame seeds
2 T. vegetable oil
1 can bean sprouts
1 can baby corn, drained
1 red pepper, thinly sliced
1 carrot, cut in strips

Sauce:
2 tsp. rice wine vinegar
1 T. light soy sauce
Dash chili oil

Mix chicken with soy sauce and sesame oil. Sprinkle with sesame seeds and let stand for 20 minutes. Discard marinade and cut chicken into thin strips. Heat oil in pan and stir-fry chicken for 4-5 minutes. Remove and let cool. Add bean sprouts, corn, pepper and carrot. Stir-fry for 2 minutes. Remove and let cool. Arrange chicken and vegetables on plate. Pour sauce over salad.

Chicken Salad

3 c. cubed cooked chicken
1 ½ c. red seedless grapes
1 c. sliced green olives
½ c. chopped walnuts
1 c. mayonnaise
½ tsp. salt

Combine all ingredients together. Chill.

Chicken & Orzo Salad

½ lb. orzo
1 T. salt
1 tomato, chopped
2 T. basil
2 T. parsley
2 T. olive oil
 1 T. lemon juice
Dash salt & black pepper
1 c. bite-size chicken, cooked

Bring pot of water to boil; add 1 tablespoon salt and orzo.
Drain. Add tomato, basil and parsley to orzo. Mix in olive oil,
lemon juice, salt and black pepper. Mix orzo with chicken.

Leftover Chicken Salad

2 c. cooked chicken, sliced
2-3 scallions, chopped
2 sour pickles, diced
¼ – ½ c. mayonnaise
Dash salt & pepper
1 tsp. pickle juice

Combine all ingredients. Serve on bed of lettuce.

Dijon Chicken Salad

1 bag lettuce
4 boneless chicken breasts
2 T. Dijon mustard
3 garlic cloves, crushed
1 T. chopped onion
4 T. white wine

Dressing:
2 T. tarragon vinegar
1 tsp. Dijon mustard
1 tsp. honey
5-6 T. olive oil

Combine chicken with all ingredients except lettuce. Marinate overnight. Bake at 350° for 35 minutes and let cool. Slice in strips or cubes. In bowl, combine lettuce and chicken. Pour dressing over salad just before serving.

Grilled Chicken Salad

1 lb. boneless chicken breast
5 c. romaine lettuce
1 c. sliced mushrooms
1 c. cherry tomatoes
½ c. croutons

Dressing:
½ c. olive oil
¼ c. Dijon mustard
2 T. lemon juice
2 tsp. Worcestershire sauce
1 tsp. grated lemon peel
1 clove garlic, minced
½ tsp. sugar
¼ tsp. ground black pepper

In bowl, whisk together dressing ingredients. Pour part of dressing over chicken; marinate for 1 hour. Remove chicken; grill for 10-15 minutes; cut in strips. Combine chicken, lettuce, mushrooms and tomatoes and toss with rest of dressing. Scatter croutons on top.

Grilled Chicken Salad
with Chow Mein

1 pkg. chicken cutlets, cubed
1 T. honey
1 T. Dijonnaise
½ c. oil
½ c. lemon juice
½ tsp. curry powder
¼ tsp. pepper
¼ tsp. salt
1 European salad mix
1 red pepper, cut in strips
1 yellow pepper, cut in strips
1 green pepper, cut in strips
1 box grape tomatoes
¼ bag chow mein noodles

Dressing:
3 T. soy sauce
¼ c. oil
¼ c. sugar
¼ c. vinegar
4 garlic cloves, crushed

Mix dressing ingredients and pour over chicken. Bake at 400°
for 20-25 minutes. Combine vegetables with chicken in bowl.
Pour dressing over and garnish with chow mein noodles on top.

Turkey Salad

½ - ¾ c. shredded turkey breast
1 bag lettuce
1 box grape tomatoes

Dressing:
4 T. mayonnaise
2 tsp. mustard
1 ½ tsp. sugar
Sprinkle garlic powder
Sprinkle black pepper

Combine together turkey, lettuce and tomatoes. Pour dressing
over just before serving.

Turkey Salad

1 lb. smoked turkey
2 bags romaine lettuce
2 tomatoes, cubed

Dressing:
¼ c. olive oil
2 cloves garlic
1 T. lemon juice
3 drops teriyaki sauce
3 T. mayonnaise
2 tsp. chopped parsley
½ tsp. dry mustard

Combine turkey, lettuce and tomatoes. Whisk dressing ingredients together. Pour dressing over salad just before serving.

Turkey Roll Salad

1 pkg. turkey roll
1 pkg. turkey pastrami
4 sour pickles, diced
Mayonnaise
Garlic powder
Crackers

Cube both packages of meat; add in pickles. Add mayonnaise and garlic powder to taste. Serve with crackers.

Dips & Dressings

Avocado Dip

1 avocado, peeled & finely chopped
2 T. mayonnaise
4 hard-boiled eggs
1 tsp. grated onion
Salt & pepper to taste

Mix ingredients in blender.

Celery Dip

5 celery stalks
1 bunch fresh parsley
1 bunch fresh dill
5 garlic cloves
¼ — ½ c. mayonnaise

Mix ingredients in food processor until smooth.

Creamy Dressing

¾ c. sugar
1 ⅓ c oil
⅔ c. vinegar
6 T. mayonnaise
3 garlic cloves
Salt & pepper
1 tsp. dry mustard
1 T. poppy seed

Blend all ingredients in blender.

Dip

1 c. mayonnaise
1 bunch scallions
1 T. lemon peel

Blend ingredients in blender.

Dressing

¼ c. water
2 cloves garlic
¼ c. sugar
¼ c vinegar
1 c. mayonnaise

Blend ingredients in blender.

Greek Dip (Dairy)

1 cucumber
1 bunch scallions
1 c. plain yogurt
2 tsp. crushed garlic
3 T. chopped fresh mint

Cut cucumber, scallions and garlic very finely. Place yogurt in bowl and beat until smooth. Add rest of ingredients. Season with salt and black pepper. Cover and chill.

Lemon Dressing

2 tsp. sugar
1 tsp. mustard
⅓ c. lemon juice
Salt & black pepper
1 c. oil

Mix sugar, mustard, lemon juice and spices in blender. Slowly add oil at the end.

Lemon Dressing

¼ c. fresh lemon juice
¾ tsp. salt
¼ tsp. black pepper
½ c. olive oil

Blend ingredients in blender.

Dips & Dressings

Lemon Dressing

2 T. olive oil
Peel of a lemon
1 T. lemon juice
1 medium garlic clove
½ tsp. salt
½ tsp. black pepper

Whisk together ingredients in bowl.

No Fuss Salad Dressing

1 c. plain nonfat yogurt
2 T. buttermilk
2 T. reduced-calorie mayonnaise
1 T. prepared white horseradish
2 tsp. Dijon style mustard
1 T. chopped fresh parsley
1 tsp. chopped fresh dill
¼ tsp. celery seed
¼ tsp. black pepper

Mix well In medium bowl. Stores up to 4 days in the refrigerator.

Onion Dip

1 pint sour cream
1 envelope onion soup mix

Mix very well by hand.

Parsley Dip

½ pkg. fresh parsley
½ pkg. fresh dill
6 garlic cloves
4 T. mayonnaise
1 lemon, squeezed
1 tsp. salt
Drop of water

Blend ingredients in blender.

Pickle Juice Dressing

½ c. mayonnaise
¼ c. pickle juice
3 T. sugar

Mix together.

Russian Dressing

½ c. mayonnaise
½ c. ketchup
Garlic powder & paprika

Mix ingredients in a bowl by hand.

Salad Dressing

1 c. mayonnaise
1 T. sugar
½ T. soy sauce
1 T. vinegar
Crushed garlic
1 tsp. salt
1 tsp. mustard
1 tsp. black pepper

Mix ingredients in blender.

Tofu Salad Dressing

¼ lb. soft tofu
1 tsp. mustard
2 T. parsley
1 scallion
1 T. fresh lemon juice
1 T. vinegar
½ tsp. salt
1 garlic clove

Blend ingredients in blender.

Vinaigrette Dressing

3 T. wine vinegar
Salt & black pepper
⅔ c. olive oil

Whisk well. Taste and adjust seasonings.

Index of
Recipes

Index of Recipes

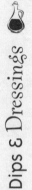

Dips & Dressings